COIN-CLUE PUZZLES

Evelyn B. Christensen

Cuisenaire Company of America, Inc.
Parsippany, New Jersey

This book is dedicated to my wonderful family and to the Ultimate Problem Solver.

Executive Editor: Doris Hirschhorn
Editorial Manager: Patsy Norvell
Development Editor: Joan Lewis
Production/Manufacturing Director: Janet Yearian
Production/Manufacturing Manager: Karen Edmonds
Production/Manufacturing Coordinator: Lorraine Allen
Design Director: Jim O'Shea
Text and Cover Design: Monika Popowitz
Composition: Joe Conte

This book is published by Cuisenaire Company
of America, Inc., an imprint of Pearson Learning.

Cuisenaire Company of America, Inc.
299 Jefferson Road
Parsippany, NJ 07054-0480

Printed in the United States of America

ISBN 1-57452-324-4
Order number 031089
1 2 3 4 5 6 7 8 9 10–ML–04 03 02 01 00

This Book Is Printed On Recycled Paper

CONTENTS

To the Problem Solver

For those of you who enjoyed my Clip-Clue Puzzles, I hope that you will find this collection of puzzles equally challenging and fun. For those of you who are new to this kind of puzzle, I welcome you to the adventure! I have had delightful fun creating these puzzles for all of you.

Object

The object of a coin-clue puzzle is to make a line of coins that satisfies all the clues.

Materials

All of the puzzles can be worked with a set of current United States coins, including: pennies, nickels, dimes, quarters, and half-dollars. The Beginning Coin-Clue Puzzles (Puzzles 1 to 30) do not use half-dollars, but the rest of the puzzles do. The maximum number of a specific coin you will need for a puzzle is eight. (You will not need more than four half-dollars for any puzzle.) You do not absolutely need the coins to solve the problems, but having physical objects to rearrange when trying to solve this type of puzzle often helps. (If coins are not available, you might use small squares of cardboard labeled with the coin values.) To record your solution to a puzzle, you may write the coin values in the given circles or you may use rubber coin stamps. If you are using the stamps, the half-dollar stamp will extend beyond the given circles, but this should not pose a problem.

Clue Clarifications

1. Each line of coins begins at the left and ends at the right.
2. Unless otherwise stated, any *number* associated with a coin refers to its monetary value. To simplify writing, the coin itself is often used to mean its monetary value. For example, a clue might say "the sum of the coins" to mean "the sum of the values of the coins."
3. The *size* of a coin refers to its diameter.

4. A *coin couple* consists of two of the same coins next to each other. If three of the same coins appear consecutively in the line, they are counted as two coin couples. If four of the same coins appear consecutively in the line, they are counted as three coin couples.

one coin couple

two coin couples

three coin couples

5. A *symmetric* line of coins is one whose coins would match if it were possible to fold the line, at its midpoint, over onto itself. This folding may include folding a coin itself in half. These are examples of symmetric lines:

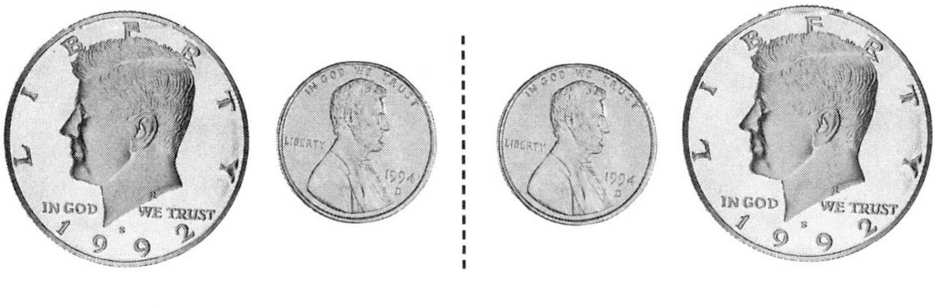

6. A line forms a *repeating pattern* if the entire line can be divided into two or more sections, all of which are identical, with the coins in the same order. These are examples:

This is not a repeating pattern:

7. Stating that a coin is *between* two specific coins does not exclude the possibility that another coin is also between those two coins. For example, in this line the dime is between two nickels; so is the quarter.

8. A *prime number* is a number (other than 1) that is divisible by only 1 and itself. Examples: 13, 17, and 29.
9. A *square number* is a number that is equal to a whole number multiplied by itself. Examples: 25, 36, and 81.

Solutions

You may verify your solutions with the answers, which begin on page 89.

You are now ready to begin the puzzles. Have fun!

Using the Puzzles

Objectives

Coin-clue puzzles are, first of all, intended to be fun, but they are also designed to help people improve their problem-solving skills. Specific skills that are developed and exercised by these puzzles include:

- analyzing relationship clues about coins
- combining information to find a solution to a problem
- recognizing when more than one solution to a problem exists
- recognizing incompatible conditions that make a problem impossible to solve
- discovering redundant information
- writing precise, creative clues about coin relationships
- evaluating solutions to determine if they meet the given criteria

These puzzles also give problem solvers the opportunity to use their knowledge of money, sums, products, differences, multiples, fractions, prime numbers, square numbers, divisibility of numbers, and averages.

Age Level of Puzzles

The activities in this book range in difficulty from easy to challenging and are appropriate for ages eight to adult. Suggestions for using the material with the lower end of the age range are given below.

Using the Puzzles with Younger Problem Solvers

For a problem-solving activity to be mind-stretching and rewarding, the problem solver must be challenged but not too frustrated. Some of the activities in this book can be quite challenging even for adults. If you are using the difficult puzzles with younger problem solvers, you may want to use one or more of these suggestions.

1. Use the puzzles with superfluous clues (Puzzles 91 to 120) as plain coin-clue puzzles. If students want to try to find superfluous clues as an extra challenge, encourage them to do so, but do not expect the class as a whole to be successful with this challenge.
2. Use Puzzles 121 to 160 as plain coin-clue puzzles, but warn the students that some will be impossible. If you want to tell them which puzzles have more than one solution, they will be more likely to find both solutions. (Otherwise, they will have the tendency to stop as soon as they find one solution.)
3. Working in groups is a good way for younger students to be successful with the more challenging puzzles in the book. Some suggestions for approaches to group activities are listed under the heading "Solving the Puzzles in Cooperative Groups."

Strategies for Using the Puzzles in a Classroom

1. Make photocopies of the pages and give an appropriate number of puzzles to students, either individually or in groups, to solve during a specific class time or as homework. If you are sending the puzzles home with students, you may wish to consider the possibility of encouraging them to involve their families in the problem-solving process.

2. Post several of the easier puzzles or one of the harder puzzles on the bulletin board and provide a box for students' solutions. Plan a time to discuss the results with the class or at least post a copy of the correct solutions.

3. Copy the puzzles on card stock and laminate them. Place these at an activity center where students who complete their regular assignments early can go and work. Solutions can be provided for them to check their own work, either on the back of each puzzle card or in an answer folder.

4. To use the puzzles when you have an extra few minutes at the end of a class period, you can show a puzzle on an overhead projector or display a sheet of newsprint on which you have previously copied a puzzle. If the clues are short you can dictate them to the students or write them on the board. Be sure to tell students the number of coins in the line.

Solving the Puzzles in Cooperative Groups

1. Use the first 60 puzzles to encourage cooperative problem solving. Here is one approach.

   - Select a puzzle.
   - Write each of the clues on a separate card without the clue numbers. Give the number of coins needed in the puzzle as an additional clue.
   - Form a group with as many problem solvers as you have clue cards. Give each problem solver a card. Give the group as a whole a set of coins and paper for recording their answer.
   - The group then works together to solve the puzzle.

   Since each person has necessary information to contribute, each person is an integral part of the problem-solving process. No one person can solve the puzzle alone.

   In a regular class you might have eight or ten small groups working simultaneously. When one group finishes a puzzle, that puzzle can be passed on to another group of the same size.

2. If students have difficulty finding both solutions to coin-clue puzzles with insufficient clues, you can use another small group approach.

   - Provide a copy of the puzzle for each member of the group and direct each one to work on the puzzle independently for five to ten minutes first.
   - Then have the members pool their solutions.
   - If the group has still not discovered two solutions, they can then work through the puzzle together verbalizing their thought processes. Several students together are more likely to discover an incorrect assumption than a single student working alone.

3. For a group approach that can help students determine when a puzzle has a superfluous clue, follow these steps.

   - Select a puzzle with three clues.
   - Divide the class into three groups and give each group a different set of two clues (that is, 1 and 2; 1 and 3; and 2 and 3).

- Ask the groups to find all the solutions that satisfy their two clues.
- Get feedback from each group. List on the board, under each pair of clues, all the solutions for that pair.
- Compare the three lists.
  - ◆ If exactly one solution is common to all three lists, that is the unique solution to the puzzle.
  - ◆ If exactly one solution is common to all three lists and that solution is the only solution for one of the lists, the clue not included in that list is superfluous. If another list has only the one solution, then the clue not included in that list is an alternative superfluous clue.
  - ◆ If more than one solution is common to all three lists, all the common solutions are solutions to the puzzle.
  - ◆ If no solution is common to all three lists, the puzzle itself has no solution.
- If a puzzle has four clues, use a similar process but divide the class into four groups, giving each a different set of three clues (that is, 1, 2, and 3; 1, 2, and 4; 1, 3, and 4; and 2, 3, and 4).

Creating Coin-Clue Puzzles

Although solving coin-clue puzzles is fun, I think creating them is even more fun. Solving a puzzle is largely an analytical, left-brain process, whereas developing a coin-clue puzzle allows a person to use the creativity of the right brain and incorporate it with the precision of the left brain—definitely a satisfying experience.

After you have introduced coin-clue puzzles to your class at school or your children at home, you are likely to have at least some individuals who are eager to try creating their own puzzles. This is a wonderful opportunity for you to encourage students' creativity. To help them be as successful as possible in their attempts, have them work at least some of the puzzles with two solutions (Puzzles 61 to 90) before they try creating an entire puzzle. These puzzles will give students practice in writing clues that distinguish between just two specific chains.

Be encouraging, not critical, of student puzzle-writing attempts. If a clue is unclear, explain why it is unclear and ask them to rewrite it. If the puzzle was intended to have a unique solution but somebody else discovers more than one solution, simply point out that the puzzle is similar to Coin-Clue Puzzles with Two Solutions and ask the creator to add another clue or clues.

Puzzles generated by your students can be posted on the bulletin board, included on student worksheets, added to the set of cards at an activity center, or discussed in an all-class, problem-solving session. Having their puzzles included with the other puzzles can be very motivating for students.

At home, you can post puzzles created by your child on the refrigerator for other family members to try solving. You can e-mail them or send them with letters to out-of-town friends or relatives. You can include them in a parent's or sibling's lunch box or exchange them with a friend who also enjoys coin-clue puzzles.

The important thing in either case is to give the creators a chance to share their puzzles with others.

Beginning Coin-Clue Puzzles

The coin-clue puzzles in this section use pennies, nickels, dimes, and quarters, but no half-dollars. The puzzles require all the given clues to determine their solutions, and each puzzle has only one solution. If you have questions about the meaning of a clue, the information in "To the Problem Solver," pages 5–8, should provide clarification.

COIN-CLUE PUZZLE 1

CLUE 1: The line is worth 25¢.
CLUE 2: The first two coins are the same.

COIN-CLUE PUZZLE 2

CLUE 1: The value of the line is 12¢.
CLUE 2: The line is symmetric.

COIN-CLUE PUZZLE 3

CLUE 1: The value of the line is 45¢.
CLUE 2: The line contains no coin couples.

COIN-CLUE PUZZLE 4

CLUE 1: The value of the line is 31¢.
CLUE 2: The coins in the line increase in value.

COIN-CLUE PUZZLE 5

CLUE 1: The line is worth 41¢.
CLUE 2: The coins are in alphabetical order.

COIN-CLUE PUZZLE 6

CLUE 1: The line is worth 20¢.
CLUE 2: The first coin is the smallest in size.

COIN-CLUE PUZZLE 7

CLUE 1: The sum of the first two coins is 20¢.
CLUE 2: The line is symmetric.

COIN-CLUE PUZZLE 8

CLUE 1: The value of the line is 35¢.
CLUE 2: The last coin is worth the most.

COIN-CLUE PUZZLE 9

CLUE 1: The sum of the first and last coins is 26¢.
CLUE 2: The coins in the line decrease in size.

COIN-CLUE PUZZLE 10

CLUE 1: The line is worth 21¢.
CLUE 2: The sum of the first and third coins equals the last coin.

COIN-CLUE PUZZLE 11

CLUE 1: The value of the line is 36¢.
CLUE 2: The coins increase in size.

COIN-CLUE PUZZLE 12

CLUE 1: The sum of all the coins is 45¢.
CLUE 2: The coins are in alphabetical order.

COIN-CLUE PUZZLE 13

CLUE 1: The value of the line is more than 51¢ and less than 60¢.
CLUE 2: The line is symmetric.

COIN-CLUE PUZZLE 14

CLUE 1: The sum of all the coins is 40¢.
CLUE 2: Each coin is the same size or smaller than the one before it.

COIN-CLUE PUZZLE 15

CLUE 1: The line is worth between 10¢ and 30¢.
CLUE 2: The line contains two coin couples.

COIN-CLUE PUZZLE 16

CLUE 1: The difference between the first two coins is 20¢.

CLUE 2: The difference between the last two coins is 5¢.

COIN-CLUE PUZZLE 17

CLUE 1: The first two coins are worth 4¢ less than the last two.

CLUE 2: The last two coins are a coin couple.

COIN-CLUE PUZZLE 18

CLUE 1: The value of the line is more than 15¢ and less than 20¢.

CLUE 2: The coins are in order from greatest value to least value.

COIN-CLUE PUZZLE 19

CLUE 1: The sum of the first two coins is 26¢.
CLUE 2: The sum of the last two coins is 35¢.

COIN-CLUE PUZZLE 20

CLUE 1: The line is worth less than 22¢.
CLUE 2: No nickels are in the line.
CLUE 3: The line is symmetric.

COIN-CLUE PUZZLE 21

CLUE 1: The value of the line is 36¢.
CLUE 2: Each coin is worth the same as or more than the coin after it.

COIN-CLUE PUZZLE 22

CLUE 1: The sum of all the coins is 16¢.
CLUE 2: The last two coins are worth 5¢ more than the first two.

COIN-CLUE PUZZLE 23

CLUE 1: The value of the line is 30¢.
CLUE 2: The line is a repeating pattern.
CLUE 3: The first coin is worth less than the last coin.

COIN-CLUE PUZZLE 24

CLUE 1: The line is worth 22¢.
CLUE 2: The first coin is smaller in size than the second coin.
CLUE 3: The line is symmetric.

COIN-CLUE PUZZLE 25

CLUE 1: The coins in the line increase in size.
CLUE 2: The first coin is worth twice the last coin.

COIN-CLUE PUZZLE 26

CLUE 1: The difference between the first two coins is 15¢.
CLUE 2: The sum of the first and last coins is 50¢.

COIN-CLUE PUZZLE 27

CLUE 1: The line has two coin couples.
CLUE 2: The first half of the line is worth twice the last half.

COIN-CLUE PUZZLE 28

CLUE 1: The value of the line is 31¢.
CLUE 2: The line is symmetric.
CLUE 3: The last coin does not have a ridged edge.

COIN-CLUE PUZZLE 29

CLUE 1: The value of the line is an odd number.
CLUE 2: The sum of the middle two coins is 6¢.
CLUE 3: Each coin is worth the same as or more than the coin before it.

COIN-CLUE PUZZLE 30

CLUE 1: The value of the line is a multiple of 7.
CLUE 2: Only the first coin has a ridged edge.
CLUE 3: The value of the line is an even number.

More for Your Money

The coin-clue puzzles in this section use pennies, nickels, dimes, quarters, and half-dollars. Just as in the Beginning Coin-Clue Puzzles, these puzzles require all the given clues to determine their solutions, and each puzzle has only one solution. Most of these puzzles are a little more difficult than those in the first section.

COIN-CLUE PUZZLE 31

CLUE 1: The value of the line is 85¢.
CLUE 2: Each coin is the same size or bigger than the one before it.

COIN-CLUE PUZZLE 32

CLUE 1: The sum of all the coins is 56¢.
CLUE 2: The coins are in alphabetical order.

COIN-CLUE PUZZLE 33

CLUE 1: The line is worth 80¢.
CLUE 2: The coins are in order from greatest value to least value.

COIN-CLUE PUZZLE 34

CLUE 1: The sum of all the coins is 52¢.
CLUE 2: The line is symmetric.

COIN-CLUE PUZZLE 35

CLUE 1: The value of the line is 90¢.
CLUE 2: Each coin is the same size or bigger than the one after it.

COIN-CLUE PUZZLE 36

CLUE 1: The line is worth 81¢.
CLUE 2: The coins increase in value.

COIN-CLUE PUZZLE 37

CLUE 1: The value of the line is 56¢.
CLUE 2: The last coin is worth more than 5¢.
CLUE 3: The largest and smallest coins in the line are next to each other.

COIN-CLUE PUZZLE 38

CLUE 1: The middle coin is the sum of the first and last coins.
CLUE 2: The smallest-sized coin is not in the line.

COIN-CLUE PUZZLE 39

CLUE 1: The difference between the first two coins is 49¢.
CLUE 2: The difference between the last two coins is 40¢.

COIN-CLUE PUZZLE 40

CLUE 1: The first coin is worth five times the second coin.
CLUE 2: The difference between the last two coins is 20¢.

COIN-CLUE PUZZLE 41

CLUE 1: The value of the line is 65¢.
CLUE 2: The line has no coin couples.
CLUE 3: The smallest-sized coin is first.

COIN-CLUE PUZZLE 42

CLUE 1: The second coin is worth half the first coin.
CLUE 2: The last coin is worth ten times the second coin.

COIN-CLUE PUZZLE 43

CLUE 1: The first two coins are worth 75¢.
CLUE 2: The last two coins are worth 55¢.
CLUE 3: The second coin is next to two of the same coins.

COIN-CLUE PUZZLE 44

CLUE 1: The middle coin is worth five times the last coin.
CLUE 2: The last coin is worth five times the first coin.

COIN-CLUE PUZZLE 45

CLUE 1: The value is greater than 5¢ and less than 20¢.
CLUE 2: The last coin is worth more than the first coin.
CLUE 3: The line forms a repeating pattern.

COIN-CLUE PUZZLE 46

CLUE 1: The sum of the first two coins is more than 60¢.
CLUE 2: The sum of the last two coins is less than 30¢.

COIN-CLUE PUZZLE 47

CLUE 1: The value of the line is 71¢.
CLUE 2: The line does not have a coin couple.
CLUE 3: The sum of the first three coins is less than the last coin.

COIN-CLUE PUZZLE 48

CLUE 1: The line is a repeating pattern.
CLUE 2: The second coin is worth half the third coin.
CLUE 3: All the coins have ridged edges.

COIN-CLUE PUZZLE 49

CLUE 1: The first and last coins are the same.
CLUE 2: The sum of the first two coins is 30¢.
CLUE 3: The sum of the last two coins is 26¢.

COIN-CLUE PUZZLE 50

CLUE 1: The value of the line is greater than $1.05.
CLUE 2: The line contains only one coin couple.
CLUE 3: The sum of the first two coins equals the last coin.

COIN-CLUE PUZZLE 51

CLUE 1: All of the coins have smooth edges.
CLUE 2: The second coin is worth less than the first coin.
CLUE 3: The first coin is worth half the sum of the last two coins.

COIN-CLUE PUZZLE 52

CLUE 1: The value of the line is 81¢.
CLUE 2: The second coin is next to two of the same coins.
CLUE 3: The fourth coin is next to two of the same coins.
CLUE 4: The second coin has a ridged edge.

COIN-CLUE PUZZLE 53

CLUE 1: The average value of the coins is 20¢.
CLUE 2: The first coin has a ridged edge.
CLUE 3: Except for the fourth coin, the coins are in order from smallest value to largest.

COIN-CLUE PUZZLE 54

CLUE 1: The sum of the middle two coins is half the total value.
CLUE 2: The last coin is half the second coin.
CLUE 3: The total value is more than 30¢.

COIN-CLUE PUZZLE 55

CLUE 1: The value of the line is $1.10.
CLUE 2: The line is a repeating pattern.
CLUE 3: The first coin has a ridged edge.

COIN-CLUE PUZZLE 56

CLUE 1: The line is worth more than 80¢.
CLUE 2: The product of the last two coins equals the second coin.
CLUE 3: The line contains two coin couples.

COIN-CLUE PUZZLE 57

CLUE 1: The total value is more than 41¢ and less than 61¢.
CLUE 2: The total value is a prime number.
CLUE 3: The last coin has a ridged edge.

COIN-CLUE PUZZLE 58

CLUE 1: The total value of the line is a multiple of six.
CLUE 2: The middle two coins are a coin couple.
CLUE 3: The coins are in order by value from greatest to least.

COIN-CLUE PUZZLE 59

CLUE 1: The average value of each coin is 14¢.
CLUE 2: The last four coins form a repeating pattern.
CLUE 3: The last coin is half the value of the first coin.

COIN-CLUE PUZZLE 60

CLUE 1: The sum of the first three coins equals the last coin.
CLUE 2: The sum of the third and fourth coins equals the first.

Coin-Clue Puzzles with Two Solutions

The coin-clue puzzles in this section use pennies, nickels, dimes, quarters, and half-dollars. Unlike the puzzles in the first two sections, these puzzles do not give enough clues to have just one solution.

For each puzzle, study the clue or clues that are given. Figure out two different solutions that satisfy all the given clues.

After you have found the two solutions, record one in the first answer space and the other one in the second answer space. Then write a clue that would make the first solution the only possible answer. Next write a different clue that would make the second solution the only possible answer.

For an extra challenge, try to write a clue that still requires all the given clues to solve the puzzle. This will be more challenging for some of the puzzles than for others. You may wish to work through the Coin-Clue Puzzles with Superfluous Clues (Puzzles 91 to 120) first to give you practice in determining when a clue is unnecessary.

COIN-CLUE PUZZLE 61

CLUE 1: The value of the line is 60¢.
CLUE 2: The line is symmetric.

CLUE 3A: ______________________________

CLUE 3B: ______________________________

COIN-CLUE PUZZLE 62

CLUE 1: The first coin is the sum of the last two.

CLUE 2A: ______________________________

CLUE 2B: ______________________________

COIN-CLUE PUZZLE 63

CLUE 1: The difference between the first and last coins is 9¢.

CLUE 2: The sum of the last two coins is 11¢.

CLUE 3A: ______________________________

CLUE 3B: ______________________________

COIN-CLUE PUZZLE 64

CLUE 1: The value of the line is $1.02.

CLUE 2: The line contains no coin couples.

CLUE 3A: ______________________________

CLUE 3B: ______________________________

COIN-CLUE PUZZLE 65

CLUE 1: The sum of the first two coins is 35¢.
CLUE 2: The sum of the last two coins is 35¢.

CLUE 3A: ______________________________

CLUE 3B: ______________________________

COIN-CLUE PUZZLE 66

CLUE 1: The line increases in value.
CLUE 2: The difference between the first and last coins is 24¢.

CLUE 3A: ______________________________

CLUE 3B: ______________________________

COIN-CLUE PUZZLE 67

CLUE 1: The line is symmetric.
CLUE 2: The value of the line is between 10¢ and 15¢.

CLUE 3A: ______________________________

CLUE 3B: ______________________________

COIN-CLUE PUZZLE 68

CLUE 1: The value of the line is 55¢.
CLUE 2: The line has two coin couples.

CLUE 3A: ______________________________

CLUE 3B: ______________________________

COIN-CLUE PUZZLE 69

CLUE 1: The difference between the last two coins is 15¢.

CLUE 2: The difference between the first and last coins is zero.

CLUE 3A: ______________________________

CLUE 3B: ______________________________

COIN-CLUE PUZZLE 70

CLUE 1: A nickel is between two dimes.

CLUE 2: A penny is between a dime and a nickel.

CLUE 3A: ______________________________

CLUE 3B: ______________________________

COIN-CLUE PUZZLE 71

CLUE 1: The last coin is worth one fifth the second coin.
CLUE 2: The line is symmetric.
CLUE 3: Not all of the coins have ridged edges.

CLUE 4A: ______________________

CLUE 4B: ______________________

COIN-CLUE PUZZLE 72

CLUE 1: The line is worth 61¢.
CLUE 2: The product of the second and third coins equals the last.
CLUE 3: The line contains one or more coin couples.

CLUE 4A: ______________________

CLUE 4B: ______________________

COIN-CLUE PUZZLE 73

CLUE 1: The middle coin is worth five times the sum of the other two coins.

CLUE 2A: ____________________

CLUE 2B: ____________________

COIN-CLUE PUZZLE 74

CLUE 1: The value of the line is greater than 60¢.
CLUE 2: The line is symmetric.
CLUE 3: The second coin has a smooth edge.

CLUE 4A: ____________________

CLUE 4B: ____________________

COIN-CLUE PUZZLE 75

CLUE 1: All of the coins have smooth edges.

CLUE 2: The sum of the last two coins is less than the sum of the first two.

CLUE 3: The sum of the first and last coins is more than the sum of the middle coins.

CLUE 4A: ______________________________

CLUE 4B: ______________________________

COIN-CLUE PUZZLE 76

CLUE 1: The average value of the coins is 15¢.

CLUE 2: The line is a repeating pattern.

CLUE 3A: ______________________________

CLUE 3B: ______________________________

COIN-CLUE PUZZLE 77

CLUE 1: The sum of the first two coins is 55¢.
CLUE 2: The line contains a coin couple.
CLUE 3: The first coin is worth half the last coin.

CLUE 4A: ____________________

CLUE 4B: ____________________

COIN-CLUE PUZZLE 78

CLUE 1: The line is worth $1.60.
CLUE 2: The second coin is not the greatest value.
CLUE 3: The line is symmetric.

CLUE 4A: ____________________

CLUE 4B: ____________________

COIN-CLUE PUZZLE 79

CLUE 1: The value of the line is 42¢.
CLUE 2: The first coin is not smooth-edged.
CLUE 3: The smallest-sized coin is next to two coins of the same value.

CLUE 4A: ____________________

CLUE 4B: ____________________

COIN-CLUE PUZZLE 80

CLUE 1: The value of the line is a square number.
CLUE 2: The line does not contain any nickels.

CLUE 3A: ____________________

CLUE 3B: ____________________

COIN-CLUE PUZZLE 81

CLUE 1: The line is symmetric.
CLUE 2: The line contains fewer than two coin couples.
CLUE 3: All the coins in the line have smooth edges.

CLUE 4A: ______________________________

CLUE 4B: ______________________________

COIN-CLUE PUZZLE 82

CLUE 1: The line is worth 50¢.
CLUE 2: The line contains exactly two coin couples.
CLUE 3: The line is a repeating pattern.

CLUE 4A: ______________________________

CLUE 4B: ______________________________

COIN-CLUE PUZZLE 83

CLUE 1: A half-dollar is between a quarter and a dime.
CLUE 2: Neither nickel is first in line.
CLUE 3: A penny is four coins from a quarter.
CLUE 4: Neither of the middle two coins has a smooth edge.

CLUE 5A: ______________________________

CLUE 5B: ______________________________

COIN-CLUE PUZZLE 84

CLUE 1: The line is worth 45¢.
CLUE 2: No coin is next to two coins of the same value.

CLUE 3A: ______________________________

CLUE 3B: ______________________________

COIN-CLUE PUZZLE 85

CLUE 1: The sum of the middle two coins equals the sixth coin.
CLUE 2: The line contains three coin couples.
CLUE 3: The second coin is worth 15¢ less than the third coin.

CLUE 4A: ______________________________

CLUE 4B: ______________________________

COIN-CLUE PUZZLE 86

CLUE 1: The line is symmetric.
CLUE 2: The sum of the first three coins is 70¢.
CLUE 3: The line contains two coin couples.

CLUE 4A: ______________________________

CLUE 4B: ______________________________

COIN-CLUE PUZZLE 87

CLUE 1: A nickel is between two dimes.
CLUE 2: A penny is between two nickels.
CLUE 3: A dime is between two pennies.
CLUE 4: The fourth coin minus the third coin equals 9¢.

CLUE 5A: ______________________

CLUE 5B: ______________________

COIN-CLUE PUZZLE 88

CLUE 1: The line contains three coin couples.
CLUE 2: The sum of the third and fourth coins is 15¢.

CLUE 3A: ______________________

CLUE 3B: ______________________

COIN-CLUE PUZZLE 89

CLUE 1: The line is worth 51¢.
CLUE 2: A penny is between a nickel and a quarter.
CLUE 3: A dime is between a quarter and a penny.
CLUE 4: The two cheapest coins are between two coins of the same value.

CLUE 5A: ____________________

CLUE 5B: ____________________

COIN-CLUE PUZZLE 90

CLUE 1: The second coin minus the first coin equals the third coin.
CLUE 2: The sum of the last two coins equals the second coin.

CLUE 3A: ____________________

CLUE 3B: ____________________

Coin-Clue Puzzles with Superfluous Clues

The coin-clue puzzles in this section use pennies, nickels, dimes, quarters, and half-dollars.

Some of the coin-clue puzzles in this section have an extra clue that is not needed to find the unique solution to the puzzle. This superfluous clue adds no information to that already known from the rest of the clues.

For each puzzle find the unique solution, then check the clues to see if any of them are superfluous. If you find a superfluous clue, draw a circle around it. Some puzzles will have one superfluous clue, some will have two alternative superfluous clues, and some will have no superfluous clues.

COIN-CLUE PUZZLE 91

CLUE 1: The line is worth 80¢.
CLUE 2: The half-dollar is next to two coins of the same value.
CLUE 3: The sum of the first two coins is 20¢.

COIN-CLUE PUZZLE 92

CLUE 1: The value of the line is more than 60¢.
CLUE 2: The line is symmetric.
CLUE 3: The line does not include a half-dollar.

COIN-CLUE PUZZLE 93

CLUE 1: The value of the line is a multiple of 11.
CLUE 2: The sum of the last two coins is an even number less than 26.
CLUE 3: Each coin is worth less than the coin before it.

COIN-CLUE PUZZLE 94

CLUE 1: The average value of the coins is 10¢.
CLUE 2: The line has exactly two coin couples.
CLUE 3: The last two coins are the same value.

COIN-CLUE PUZZLE 95

CLUE 1: A half-dollar comes between a nickel and a dime.
CLUE 2: A penny comes after the dime.
CLUE 3: A nickel is not next to the half-dollar.

COIN-CLUE PUZZLE 96

CLUE 1: The average value of the coins is 20¢.
CLUE 2: The sum of the first two coins is 40¢ more than the last coin.

COIN-CLUE PUZZLE 97

CLUE 1: The sum of the first three coins equals the last coin.
CLUE 2: The line contains a coin couple.
CLUE 3: The coins are in alphabetical order.

COIN-CLUE PUZZLE 98

CLUE 1: The line is worth $1.10.
CLUE 2: The coins are in order from smallest value to largest value.
CLUE 3: The line has exactly one coin couple.

COIN-CLUE PUZZLE 99

CLUE 1: The average value of the coins is 2¢.
CLUE 2: The third coin is worth 2¢ more than the sum of the other coins.

COIN-CLUE PUZZLE 100

CLUE 1: The sum of the first two coins is 10¢.
CLUE 2: The coins are in order from least value to most value.
CLUE 3: The last coin is worth 10 times the middle coin.

COIN-CLUE PUZZLE 101

CLUE 1: The nickel comes after the penny.
CLUE 2: The dime comes before the quarter.
CLUE 3: The nickel is not first or last.
CLUE 4: The penny comes after the dime.

COIN-CLUE PUZZLE 102

CLUE 1: The average value of the coins is 7¢.
CLUE 2: The third and fourth coins form the only coin couple.
CLUE 3: The second coin has a ridged edge.

COIN-CLUE PUZZLE 103

CLUE 1: The value of the line is a square number.
CLUE 2: The sum of the middle two coins is 15¢ less than the last coin.
CLUE 3: The coins are in order from smallest value to greatest value.

COIN-CLUE PUZZLE 104

CLUE 1: The average value of the coins is 12¢.
CLUE 2: The sum of the last two coins is a prime number.
CLUE 3: The sum of the first two coins is a multiple of seven.

COIN-CLUE PUZZLE 105

CLUE 1: The line is worth 65¢.
CLUE 2: The line does not have exactly one coin couple.
CLUE 3: The coins are in order from least value to greatest value.

COIN-CLUE PUZZLE 106

CLUE 1: A nickel is between two dimes.
CLUE 2: The fourth coin equals the product of the two adjacent coins.
CLUE 3: The last coin minus the third coin equals the first coin.

COIN-CLUE PUZZLE 107

CLUE 1: The line is worth 30¢.
CLUE 2: The line is symmetric.
CLUE 3: The sum of the last two coins is 15¢.
CLUE 4: A smooth-edged coin is not first.

COIN-CLUE PUZZLE 108

CLUE 1: The line is in order from smallest value to largest value.
CLUE 2: The second coin divided by the first equals the last coin divided by the third.
CLUE 3: The line has more than two kinds of coins.
CLUE 4: The value of the third coin is a square number.

COIN-CLUE PUZZLE 109

CLUE 1: Both nickels come before the penny.
CLUE 2: The quarter comes after the dime.
CLUE 3: The penny comes before the quarter.
CLUE 4: The line contains no coin couple.

COIN-CLUE PUZZLE 110

CLUE 1: The average value of the coins is 15¢.
CLUE 2: The line is not symmetric.
CLUE 3: The line is not a repeating pattern.
CLUE 4: The second coin is worth more than the last coin.

COIN-CLUE PUZZLE 111

CLUE 1: The line is worth 90¢.
CLUE 2: The first coin is worth half of the second.
CLUE 3: The third coin is worth half of the fourth.
CLUE 4: The coins are not in order by value.

COIN-CLUE PUZZLE 112

CLUE 1: The line is worth 85¢.
CLUE 2: The third coin has the least value in the line.
CLUE 3: The line contains exactly one coin couple.
CLUE 4: The last coin is one fifth the first coin.

COIN-CLUE PUZZLE 113

CLUE 1: The value of the line is a prime number less than 31.
CLUE 2: The line has two coin couples.
CLUE 3: The third coin is not next to two of the same coins.
CLUE 4: The second coin has a smooth edge.

COIN-CLUE PUZZLE 114

CLUE 1: The line contains four different coins.
CLUE 2: The sum of the middle two coins is 30¢.
CLUE 3: The last coin is smaller in value than the first coin.
CLUE 4: The product of the first two coins is the product of the last two.

COIN-CLUE PUZZLE 115

CLUE 1: The average value of the coins is 14¢.
CLUE 2: The sum of the second and third coins is a multiple of six.
CLUE 3: The first four coins form a repeating pattern.
CLUE 4: The last coin is worth less than the second coin.

COIN-CLUE PUZZLE 116

CLUE 1: The value of the line is greater than 35¢.
CLUE 2: The line contains three coin couples.
CLUE 3: The difference between the third and fourth coins is 5¢.
CLUE 4: The first coin is greater in value than the last coin.

COIN-CLUE PUZZLE 117

CLUE 1: The average value of the coins is 20¢.
CLUE 2: The middle coin is next to two of the same coins.
CLUE 3: The last coin is less valuable than the first.
CLUE 4: The middle coin is less valuable than the last.

COIN-CLUE PUZZLE 118

CLUE 1: The sum of the first two coins is three times the last coin.
CLUE 2: The third coin is not next to two coins of the same value.
CLUE 3: The third coin is worth twice as much as the second coin.
CLUE 4: The first coin is worth less than the second coin.

COIN-CLUE PUZZLE 119

CLUE 1: The product of the second and fourth coins equals the third.
CLUE 2: The line is symmetric.
CLUE 3: The product of the first two coins equals the fourth.
CLUE 4: The line contains no coin couples.

COIN-CLUE PUZZLE 120

CLUE 1: The line is worth 85¢.
CLUE 2: The line has a coin couple, but not in the first two places.
CLUE 3: The second half of the line is worth more than the first half.
CLUE 4: The first coin is not a multiple of the third coin.

The Most for Your Money

The coin-clue puzzles in this section use pennies, nickels, dimes, quarters, and half-dollars.

The section contains a mixture of four different coin-clue puzzle types. For each puzzle, decide which kind it is and solve it.

Some puzzles have a contradiction between the clues that makes the puzzle impossible to solve. Mark a large X beside the puzzle if it is impossible.

Some puzzles have just one solution that satisfies all the clues and, at the same time, all the given clues are necessary to find that unique solution. Solve these puzzles and record your answer on the first line of coins.

Some puzzles have just one solution that satisfies all the clues, but one of the clues is superfluous. That clue is not needed because all the other clues combine to limit the puzzle to just one solution. For these puzzles, find the unique solution, record it on the line of coins, and then circle the superfluous clue. Some puzzles have two alternate superfluous clues. In that case, circle both clues.

Some puzzles have two different solutions that satisfy all the clues. For these puzzles, record one solution on the first line of coins and the other solution on the second line. Next write a clue that would make the first solution the unique answer to the puzzle. Then write a clue that would make the second solution the unique answer.

COIN-CLUE PUZZLE 121

CLUE 1: The line is symmetric.
CLUE 2: The third coin is a nickel.
CLUE 3: The line forms a repeating pattern.

CLUE 4A: ____________________

CLUE 4B: ____________________

COIN-CLUE PUZZLE 122

CLUE 1: The line is worth 70¢.
CLUE 2: The coins are in alphabetical order.

CLUE 3A: ____________________

CLUE 3B: ____________________

COIN-CLUE PUZZLE 123

CLUE 1: The line is worth $1.10.
CLUE 2: The product of the first two coins equals the last coin.
CLUE 3: The line forms a repeating pattern.

CLUE 4A: ______________________

CLUE 4B: ______________________

COIN-CLUE PUZZLE 124

CLUE 1: The value of the line is less than a dollar.
CLUE 2: The sum of the first two coins is 60¢.
CLUE 3: The line has a coin couple.

CLUE 4A: ______________________

CLUE 4B: ______________________

COIN-CLUE PUZZLE 125

CLUE 1: The value of the line is less than 12¢.
CLUE 2: The line does not contain a nickel.
CLUE 3: The line is symmetric.

CLUE 4A: ______________________________

CLUE 4B: ______________________________

COIN-CLUE PUZZLE 126

CLUE 1: The average value of the coins is 15¢.
CLUE 2: The line forms a repeating pattern.
CLUE 3: The value of the third coin is an even number.

CLUE 4A: ______________________________

CLUE 4B: ______________________________

COIN-CLUE PUZZLE 127

CLUE 1: The line is worth 86¢.
CLUE 2: The coins are in alphabetical order.
CLUE 3: The line contains no coin couples.

CLUE 4A: ______________________________

CLUE 4B: ______________________________

COIN-CLUE PUZZLE 128

CLUE 1: The value of the line is 75¢.
CLUE 2: The sum of the last two coins is 20¢.
CLUE 3: The second coin is ten times the first.

CLUE 4A: ______________________________

CLUE 4B: ______________________________

COIN-CLUE PUZZLE 129

CLUE 1: The average value of the coins is 11¢.
CLUE 2: The first coin is the sum of the second, third, and last coins.
CLUE 3: The line contains exactly one coin couple.

CLUE 4A: ______________________

CLUE 4B: ______________________

COIN-CLUE PUZZLE 130

CLUE 1: The average value of the coins is 20¢.
CLUE 2: The second coin is next to two coins of the same value.
CLUE 3: The last coin has the highest value in the line.

CLUE 4A: ______________________

CLUE 4B: ______________________

COIN-CLUE PUZZLE 131

CLUE 1: The average value of the coins is 24¢.
CLUE 2: The line is in alphabetical order.
CLUE 3: The last coin is worth less than the first coin.

CLUE 4A: ______________________________

CLUE 4B: ______________________________

COIN-CLUE PUZZLE 132

CLUE 1: The value of the line is a square number.
CLUE 2: Each coin is of more value than the one before it.
CLUE 3: The value of the third coin is a square number.

CLUE 4A: ______________________________

CLUE 4B: ______________________________

COIN-CLUE PUZZLE 133

CLUE 1: The value of the line is 45¢.
CLUE 2: The largest-sized coin comes before the smallest-sized.
CLUE 3: The line contains no coin couples.
CLUE 4: No coin is next to two coins of the same value.

CLUE 5A: ______________________________

CLUE 5B: ______________________________

COIN-CLUE PUZZLE 134

CLUE 1: The sum of the first two coins is four times the third coin.
CLUE 2: The third coin is next to two coins of the same value.

CLUE 3A: ______________________________

CLUE 3B: ______________________________

COIN-CLUE PUZZLE 135

CLUE 1: The value of the line is 26¢.
CLUE 2: No coin is next to two coins of the same value.
CLUE 3: The second coin is worth half the first coin.
CLUE 4: The third coin is worth less than the fourth coin.

CLUE 5A: ______________________________

CLUE 5B: ______________________________

COIN-CLUE PUZZLE 136

CLUE 1: The product of the first and last coins equals the middle coin.
CLUE 2: The line has exactly one coin whose value is even.

CLUE 3A: ______________________________

CLUE 3B: ______________________________

COIN-CLUE PUZZLE 137

CLUE 1: The value of the line is 91¢.
CLUE 2: The first, third, and fifth coins are the same.
CLUE 3: The second, fourth, and last coins increase in value.
CLUE 4: The line has no coin couples.

CLUE 5A: ______________________________

CLUE 5B: ______________________________

COIN-CLUE PUZZLE 138

CLUE 1: The difference between the first and last coins is 15¢.
CLUE 2: The first two coins are worth twice the last two coins.

CLUE 3A: ______________________________

CLUE 3B: ______________________________

COIN-CLUE PUZZLE 139

CLUE 1: The dime does not touch the half-dollar.
CLUE 2: The quarter does not touch the nickel.
CLUE 3: The nickel does not touch the dime.
CLUE 4: The nickel is not last.

CLUE 5A: ____________________

CLUE 5B: ____________________

COIN-CLUE PUZZLE 140

CLUE 1: The product of the first two coins equals the third coin.
CLUE 2: The second coin times the fourth coin equals the first coin.
CLUE 3: The last two coins are not a coin couple.

CLUE 4A: ____________________

CLUE 4B: ____________________

COIN-CLUE PUZZLE 141

CLUE 1: The value of the line is 45¢.
CLUE 2: No coin is next to two coins of the same value.
CLUE 3: The first coin is greater than the sum of the rest of the coins.
CLUE 4: The line has no coin couples.

CLUE 5A: ____________________

CLUE 5B: ____________________

COIN-CLUE PUZZLE 142

CLUE 1: The middle two coins and the last two have the same sums.
CLUE 2: The difference between the first and last coins is zero.
CLUE 3: The difference between the first and third coins is 9¢.

CLUE 4A: ____________________

CLUE 4B: ____________________

COIN-CLUE PUZZLE 143

CLUE 1: The average value of the coins is 11¢.
CLUE 2: The fourth coin is the most valuable coin in the line.
CLUE 3: The line contains no coin couples.

CLUE 4A: ______________________________

CLUE 4B: ______________________________

COIN-CLUE PUZZLE 144

CLUE 1: A nickel comes next after the first 30¢ worth of coins.
CLUE 2: The line is symmetric.
CLUE 3: The line has at least one coin couple.
CLUE 4: The first coin has a ridged edge.

CLUE 5A: ______________________________

CLUE 5B: ______________________________

COIN-CLUE PUZZLE 145

CLUE 1: The value of the line is a multiple of six.
CLUE 2: The sum of the first three coins is a multiple of six.
CLUE 3: The line is in order from largest value to smallest value.
CLUE 4: The line contains exactly one coin couple.

CLUE 5A: ____________________

CLUE 5B: ____________________

COIN-CLUE PUZZLE 146

CLUE 1: The average value of the coins is 19¢.
CLUE 2: The line contains no coin couples.
CLUE 3: Neither end of the line is smooth-edged.
CLUE 4: The quarter is the third coin from the half-dollar.

CLUE 5A: ____________________

CLUE 5B: ____________________

COIN-CLUE PUZZLE 147

CLUE 1: The total value of the line is a multiple of nine.
CLUE 2: The sum of the middle two coins is one third the total of the line.
CLUE 3: The last two coins are a coin couple.

CLUE 4A: ______________________________

CLUE 4B: ______________________________

COIN-CLUE PUZZLE 148

CLUE 1: The last coin divided by the third coin equals the second coin.
CLUE 2: The first coin divided by the second coin equals the second coin.
CLUE 3: The line contains no coin couples.

CLUE 4A: ______________________________

CLUE 4B: ______________________________

COIN-CLUE PUZZLE 149

CLUE 1: The value of the line is greater than 51¢.
CLUE 2: The line is in alphabetical order.
CLUE 3: The coins are in order from smallest size to largest size.
CLUE 4: The line has exactly one coin couple.

CLUE 5A: ______________________________

CLUE 5B: ______________________________

COIN-CLUE PUZZLE 150

CLUE 1: The value of the line is a square number.
CLUE 2: The first three coins are the same.
CLUE 3: The last coin is not the same as any other coin in the line.

CLUE 4A: ______________________________

CLUE 4B: ______________________________

COIN-CLUE PUZZLE 151

CLUE 1: A dime is next to two coins of the same value.
CLUE 2: A nickel is between a penny and a quarter.
CLUE 3: A quarter is between a dime and a penny.
CLUE 4: The line has at least one coin couple.

CLUE 5A: ______________________________

CLUE 5B: ______________________________

COIN-CLUE PUZZLE 152

CLUE 1: The coins are in reverse alphabetical order.
CLUE 2: The sum of the first two coins times the third coin equals the last coin.

CLUE 3A: ______________________________

CLUE 3B: ______________________________

COIN-CLUE PUZZLE 153

CLUE 1: Both dimes touch a penny and a nickel.
CLUE 2: A nickel is next to two coins of the same value.
CLUE 3: The fourth coin is worth less than the fifth coin.
CLUE 4: The line has a coin couple.

CLUE 5A: ____________________

CLUE 5B: ____________________

COIN-CLUE PUZZLE 154

CLUE 1: The sum of the middle two coins is less than the last coin.
CLUE 2: The sum of the first two coins is 15¢ more than the sum of the last two coins.

CLUE 3A: ____________________

CLUE 3B: ____________________

COIN-CLUE PUZZLE 155

CLUE 1: A dime comes next after the first 85¢ worth of coins.
CLUE 2: A quarter comes before a half-dollar.
CLUE 3: The second coin is next to two coins of the same value.
CLUE 4: The quarter is not next to a dime.

CLUE 5A: ______________________________

CLUE 5B: ______________________________

COIN-CLUE PUZZLE 156

CLUE 1: The value of the line is a square number.
CLUE 2: The line is symmetric.
CLUE 3: The line has two or less coin couples.

CLUE 4A: ______________________________

CLUE 4B: ______________________________

COIN-CLUE PUZZLE 157

CLUE 1: The difference between the fourth and fifth coins is 15¢.
CLUE 2: The second coin is five times the last coin.
CLUE 3: The line contains three coin couples.

CLUE 4A: ______________________________

CLUE 4B: ______________________________

COIN-CLUE PUZZLE 158

CLUE 1: The average value of the coins is 15¢.
CLUE 2: The ends of the line are the same value.
CLUE 3: The fourth coin is not a dime.
CLUE 4: The line is not symmetric.
CLUE 5: The line contains no coin couples.

CLUE 6A: ______________________________

CLUE 6B: ______________________________

COIN-CLUE PUZZLE 159

CLUE 1: A dime is between a nickel and a penny.
CLUE 2: A nickel is the fourth coin from a half-dollar.
CLUE 3: The line contains a coin couple.
CLUE 4: The coins are in order from smallest value to largest value, except for the middle coin.

CLUE 5A: ______________________________

CLUE 5B: ______________________________

COIN-CLUE PUZZLE 160

CLUE 1: The value of the line is 65¢.
CLUE 2: The sum of the first two coins is less than the sum of the last two.
CLUE 3: The sum of the first and last coins is greater than the sum of the middle two coins.
CLUE 4: The sum of the second and fourth coins is greater than the sum of the first and third coins.

CLUE 5A: ______________________________

CLUE 5B: ______________________________

Solutions to Coin-Clue Puzzles

Written clues that are given as part of the answer to puzzles with two solutions will vary. Those included here are examples of clues that will not cause any of the preceding clues in the puzzle to be superfluous. (Satisfying this requirement was the "Extra Challenge," which was suggested in the section Coin-Clue Puzzles with Two Solutions.)

Beginning Coin-Clue Puzzles

1. (10) (10) (5)

2. (1) (10) (1)

3. (10) (25) (10)

4. (1) (5) (25)

5. (10) (5) (1) (25)

6. (10) (5) (5)

7. (10) (10) (10)

8. (5) (5) (25)

9. (25) (5) (1)

10. (5) (1) (5) (10)

11. (10) (1) (25)

12. (10) (5) (5) (25)

13. (25) (5) (25)

14. (25) (5) (10)

15. (5) (5) (5)

16. (25) (5) (10)

17. (1) (5) (5)

18. (10) (5) (1)

19. (1) (25) (10)

20. (1) (1) (1) (1)

21. (25) (5) (5) (1)

22. (5) (1) (10)

23. (5) (10) (5) (10)

24. (10) (1) (1) (10)

25. (10) (1) (5)

26. (25) (10) (25)

27. (10) (10) (5) (5)

28. (5) (10) (1) (10) (5)

29. (1) (1) (5) (10)

30. (25) (1) (1) (1)

More for Your Money

31.	(10)	(25)	(50)		
32.	(50)	(5)	(1)		
33.	(50)	(25)	(5)		
34.	(1)	(50)	(1)		
35.	(50)	(25)	(5)	(10)	
36.	(1)	(5)	(25)	(50)	
37.	(5)	(1)	(50)		
38.	(25)	(50)	(25)		
39.	(1)	(50)	(10)		
40.	(25)	(5)	(25)		
41.	(10)	(25)	(5)	(25)	
42.	(10)	(5)	(50)		
43.	(50)	(25)	(50)	(5)	
44.	(1)	(25)	(5)		
45.	(1)	(5)	(1)	(5)	
46.	(50)	(25)	(1)		
47.	(10)	(1)	(10)	(50)	
48.	(50)	(25)	(50)	(25)	
49.	(25)	(5)	(1)	(25)	
50.	(25)	(25)	(10)	(50)	
51.	(5)	(1)	(5)	(5)	
52.	(10)	(50)	(10)	(1)	(10)
53.	(10)	(10)	(25)	(5)	(50)
54.	(50)	(50)	(25)	(25)	
55.	(50)	(5)	(50)	(5)	
56.	(50)	(50)	(50)	(1)	
57.	(1)	(1)	(1)	(50)	
58.	(25)	(5)	(5)	(1)	
59.	(10)	(25)	(5)	(25)	(5)
60.	(10)	(10)	(5)	(5)	(25)

Coin-Clue Puzzles with Two Solutions

61.	(5)	(50)	(5)		—The first coin in the line is worth the least.
	(25)	(10)	(25)		—The middle coin in the line is worth the least.
62.	(50)	(25)	(25)		—The value of at least one coin is a square number.
	(10)	(5)	(5)		—The line does not contain a half-dollar.
63.	(1)	(1)	(10)		—The line is worth less than 20 cents.
	(10)	(10)	(1)		—The line is worth more than 15 cents.
64.	(50)	(1)	(50)	(1)	—The last coin in the line is worth the least.
	(1)	(50)	(1)	(50)	—The first coin in the line is worth the least.
65.	(25)	(10)	(25)		—The value of the first coin is a square number.
	(10)	(25)	(10)		—The line is worth less than 60 cents.
66.	(1)	(5)	(25)		—The line is worth less than 35 cents.
	(1)	(10)	(25)		—The value of one of the coins is an even number.
67.	(1)	(10)	(1)		—One of the coins has a ridged edge.
	(5)	(1)	(5)		—All of the coins have smooth edges.
68.	(25)	(10)	(10)	(10)	—The last coin is not worth the most.
	(10)	(10)	(10)	(25)	—The first coin is not worth the most.
69.	(10)	(25)	(10)		—The line is worth less than 50 cents.
	(25)	(10)	(25)		—The line is worth more than 45 cents.
70.	(10)	(5)	(1)	(10)	—The first three coins decrease in value.
	(10)	(1)	(5)	(10)	—The last three coins increase in value.
71.	(1)	(5)	(5)	(1)	—The line does not contain a quarter.
	(5)	(25)	(25)	(5)	—The line does not contain a penny.
72.	(10)	(1)	(25)	(25)	—The first coin is not worth the most.
	(50)	(1)	(5)	(5)	—The first coin is worth the most.
73.	(1)	(10)	(1)		—The sum of the first two coins is a prime number.
	(5)	(50)	(5)		—The sum of the first two coins is divisible by 5.
74.	(50)	(5)	(5)	(50)	—The line does not contain a penny.
	(50)	(1)	(1)	(50)	—The line does not contain a nickel.
75.	(5)	(1)	(1)	(1)	—The line has two coin couples.
	(5)	(5)	(1)	(5)	—The line has exactly one coin couple.

76. (25) (5) (25) (5) —The first coin is worth 5 times the last coin.
(5) (25) (5) (25) —The third coin has a smooth edge.

77. (5) (50) (50) (10) —The third coin is worth more than the fourth.
(5) (50) (10) (10) —The second coin is worth more than the third.

78. (50) (5) (50) (5) (50) —The line contains only two kinds of coins.
(50) (25) (10) (25) (50) —The line contains exactly three kinds of coins.

79. (25) (5) (1) (10) (1) —The last coin is worth the least.
(25) (1) (10) (1) (5) —The middle three coins are symmetric.

80. (1) (1) (1) (1) —The line contains a smooth-edged coin.
(25) (25) (25) (25) —The line is worth more than 20 cents.

81. (1) (5) (1) (5) (1) —The value of the last coin is a square number.
(5) (1) (5) (1) (5) —The first two coins are in alphabetical order.

82. (10) (10) (5) (10) (10) (5) —The first coin has a ridged edge.
(5) (10) (10) (5) (10) (10) —The value of the third coin is an even number.

83. (25) (5) (50) (10) (1) (5) —The third coin is worth more than the fourth.
(1) (5) (10) (50) (25) (5) —The first coin is worth less than the last.

84. (10) (5) (5) (10) (10) (5) —The first half of the line is worth less than the second half.
(5) (10) (10) (5) (5) (10) —The middle two coins are in alphabetical order.

85. (10) (10) (25) (25) (25) (50) —A coin is next to two coins of the same value.
(10) (10) (25) (25) (50) (50) —The line is worth more than $1.50.

86. (50) (10) (10) (10) (50) —The line is worth more than $1.00.
(10) (10) (50) (10) (10) —The first coin is the smallest-sized.

87. (10) (5) (1) (10) (5) (1) —The last coin is worth less than the fifth coin.
(10) (5) (1) (10) (1) (5) —The last coin is worth more than the fifth coin.

88. (10) (10) (10) (5) (5) —The value of the second coin is an even number.
(5) (5) (5) (10) (10) —The line is worth less than 40 cents.

89. (10) (5) (1) (10) (25) —The second coin has a smooth edge.
(25) (10) (1) (5) (10) —The second coin is worth more than the fourth.

90. (5) (10) (5) (5) —The value of a coin is a prime number.
(25) (50) (25) (25) —The value of a coin is a square number.

Coin-Clue Puzzles with Superfluous Clues

91.	(10)	(10)	(50)	(10)		(clue 1)
92.	(25)	(25)	(25)			(clue 2)
93.	(50)	(10)	(5)	(1)		(clue 2)
94.	(25)	(5)	(5)	(5)		
95.	(10)	(50)	(1)	(5)		
96.	(25)	(25)	(10)			(clue 1)
97.	(10)	(10)	(5)	(25)		(clue 2)
98.	(10)	(25)	(25)	(50)		
99.	(1)	(1)	(5)	(1)		(clue 1)
100.	(5)	(5)	(50)			(clue 2)
101.	(10)	(1)	(5)	(25)		
102.	(5)	(10)	(5)	(5)	(10)	(clue 3)
103.	(1)	(5)	(5)	(25)		(clue 3)
104.	(25)	(10)	(1)			(clue 1)
105.	(5)	(5)	(5)	(50)		
106.	(5)	(10)	(5)	(50)	(10)	
107.	(10)	(5)	(5)	(10)		(clue 1 or 3)
108.	(5)	(10)	(25)	(50)		
109.	(5)	(10)	(5)	(1)	(25)	
110.	(25)	(25)	(5)	(5)		(clue 3)
111.	(25)	(50)	(5)	(10)		
112.	(25)	(50)	(5)	(5)		(clue 2 or 3)
113.	(1)	(1)	(1)	(10)		(clue 4)
114.	(50)	(5)	(25)	(10)		
115.	(5)	(25)	(5)	(25)	(10)	(clue 2)
116.	(10)	(10)	(10)	(5)	(5)	(clue 1 or 4)
117.	(50)	(10)	(5)	(10)	(25)	
118.	(5)	(25)	(50)	(10)		(clue 2)
119.	(1)	(5)	(25)	(5)	(1)	
120.	(10)	(25)	(25)	(25)		(clue 3)

The Most for Your Money

121.	(5) (5) (5) (5)	
122.	(10) (50) (5) (5)	—Not all the coins have ridged edges.
	(10) (10) (25) (25)	—The line has two coin couples.
123.	X	
124.	(50) (10) (10)	
125.	(1) (1) (1)	(clue 3)
126.	(10) (25) (10) (10) (25) (10)	—The value of the first coin is not a square number.
	(25) (10) (10) (25) (10) (10)	—The line has two coin couples.
127.	X	
128.	(5) (50) (10) (10)	(clue 2)
129.	(25) (10) (5) (5) (10)	
130.	(10) (10) (10) (50)	—The first coin has the smallest value in the line.
	(25) (5) (25) (25)	— The line has exactly one coin couple.
131.	(10) (50) (50) (5) (5)	
132.	(1) (5) (25) (50)	(clue 3)
133.	(5) (25) (10) (5)	
134.	(10) (10) (5) (10)	—The line has a smooth-edged coin.
	(50) (50) (25) (50)	—No coin's value is a prime number.
135.	(10) (5) (1) (10)	(clue 2 or 4)
136.	X	
137.	(5) (1) (5) (25) (5) (50)	—The sixth coin is worth more than the fifth.
	(25) (1) (25) (5) (25) (10)	—The line has fewer than three smooth-edged coins.
138.	(25) (5) (10)	(clue 1)
139.	(5) (50) (25) (10)	
140.	(5) (5) (25) (1)	

141.	X	
142.	(1) (1) (10) (1)	—The line is worth less than 25 cents.
	(10) (10) (1) (10)	—The last coin is worth more than the third coin.
143.	(10) (5) (10) (25) (5)	—The first coin is worth more than the last.
	(5) (10) (5) (25) (10)	—The middle coin is worth half the last coin.
144.	(25) (5) (5) (5) (25)	(clue 3 or 4)
145.	(25) (25) (10) (5) (1)	
146.	X	
147.	(25) (10) (5) (5)	(clue 1)
148.	(25) (5) (10) (50)	
149.	X	
150.	(5) (5) (5) (10)	—The third coin is not worth more than the last coin.
	(5) (5) (5) (1)	—The value of the line is an even number.
151.	X	
152.	(1) (1) (5) (10)	—The line has exactly one coin couple.
	(5) (5) (5) (50)	—The line is worth more than 20 cents.
153.	(1) (1) (10) (5) (10) (1)	
154.	(50) (25) (10) (50)	—The first coin is worth twice the second.
	(25) (1) (1) (10)	—The line contains a coin couple.
155.	(5) (25) (5) (50) (10)	(clue 2 or 4)
156.	X	
157.	(25) (25) (25) (25) (10) (5)	—The line is worth less than $1.50.
	(50) (50) (50) (25) (10) (10)	—The line contains only coins with ridged edges.
158.	(5) (10) (5) (50) (5)	
159.	(5) (10) (1) (50) (50)	
160.	(5) (5) (5) (50)	